CW00554707

Buddhism

Eight Steps to Happiness

Buddhism

Eight Steps to Happiness

Dieter Glogowski

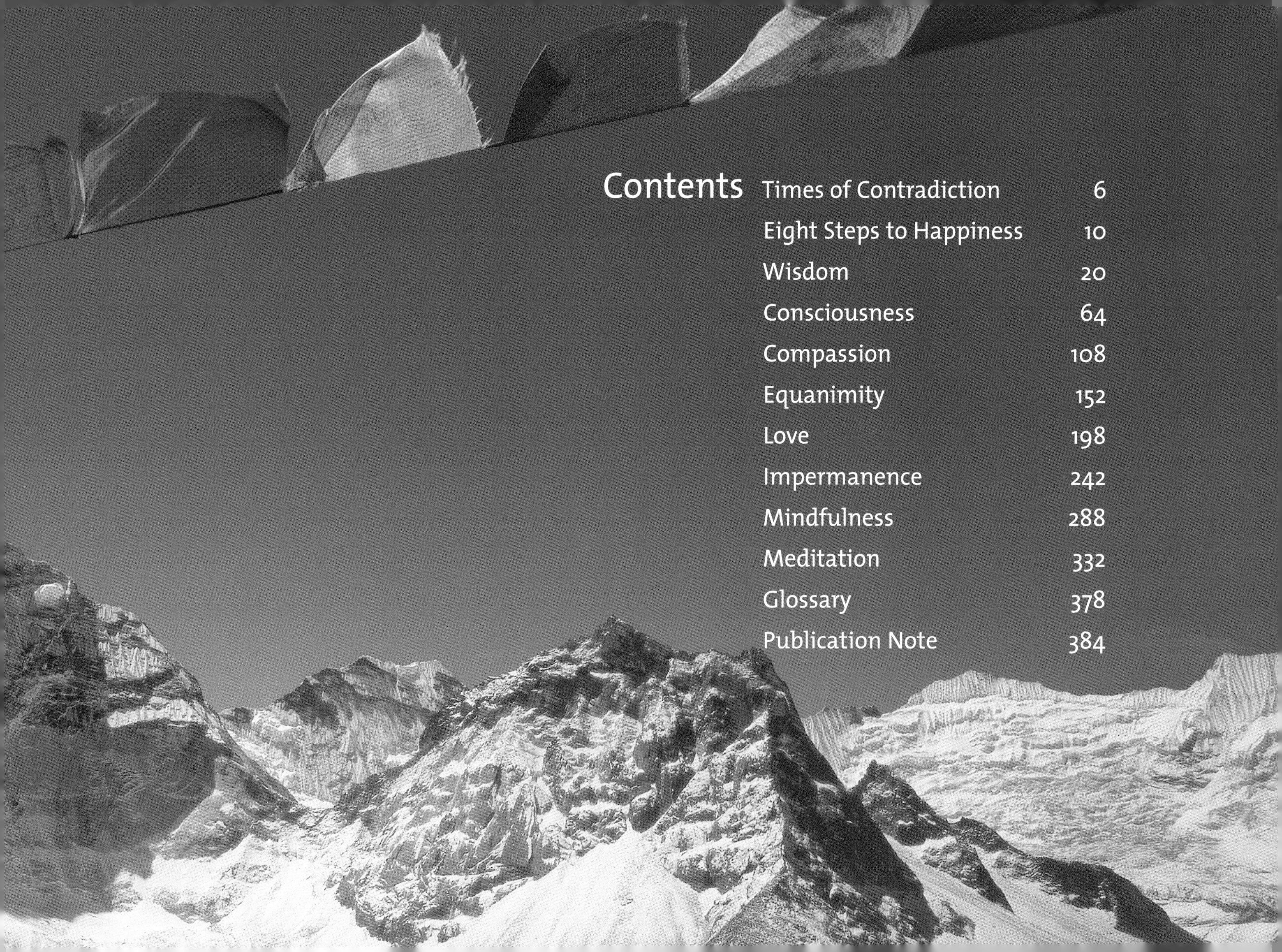

Contents

Times of Contradiction

We have larger houses, but smaller families,
more comfort, but less time.
We have more education,
but less understanding,
more knowledge, but less insight,
more experts, but more problems,
more medicine, but less good health.

We have reached the moon,
but we have problems crossing the street
to meet our new neighbors.

We invent more and more powerful computers
and produce more and more information,
for which more paper is consumed than ever before,
but there is less communication in our lives.

We get more and more in terms of quantity,
but less and less in terms of quality.
These are the times of fast food and bad digestion,
of inflated egos, but little personality,
of high profits, but superficial friendship.

These are the times of showing off
with no substantial background.

The 14th Dalai Lama

Eight Steps to Happiness

"Because this exists, that arises," the Buddha says in the Sutra of the Rice Seedling, and thus he proclaims one of the most essential teachings of Buddhism: the philosophy of dependent origination. It says that all phenomena depend on each other in terms of cause and effect, that no object, no thought, no emotion can arise out of nothing without causes and conditions. In principle, this is also valid for religions: even Buddhism itself is rooted in much older religions of ancient India. And Prince Siddhartha Gautama's awakening, which made him the Buddha, was the result of a long path of living in luxury, asceticism, and meditation.

The numerous religions and spiritual paths of this world are much more closely interlinked; they have inspired each other and exchanged substantial ideas much more than the media with their news about religious and cultural clashes would have us believe. Therefore the wise, like the 14th Dalai Lama, point out that despite their differences the essence of all religions and the basis of deepest humanity are kindness, compassion, love, and the striving for happiness and insight. Such thinking is what this book explores. Although its main focus is on the Buddhist Eightfold Noble Path, the path to enlightenment taught by the Buddha, it goes beyond the teachings of the Blessed One and collects quotations of wisdom from other religions as well.

Buddha statue in Shey Monastery, Ladakh

The Eight Steps to Happiness, which the Eightfold Noble Path could also be called, are essentially universal and as such, they transcend the boundaries of expert opinions or notions and methods of individual religions. In addition, the diagrams introducing the eight chapters of this book, known as The Eight Auspicious Symbols, are representations of archetypal meaning and cannot be restricted to a single religion. They are the wheel representing the Buddha's wisdom teachings, and the conch shell representing his speech, the vase containing the water of life and immortality, the banner of victory over ignorance, the fishes standing for love, the endless knot of eternal life, the lotus flower as a symbol of the spiritual path, and the parasol protecting from all evil.
Correspondingly the eight chapter headlines refer to aspects of a universal spiritual path: Wisdom, Consciousness, Compassion, Equanimity, Love, Impermanence, Mindfulness, Meditation – all terms that have as much meaning for a Buddhist as they do for a Christian, Muslim or Hindu, even though their meaning may slightly differ in the context of the individual religion.

The life story and the times of the Buddha as well as the history of Buddhism are examples of the interconnectedness of spiritual paths. The times in which the Buddha was born were times of spiritual transformation. Philosopher Karl Jaspers refers to such times of deep historical shift as "Achsenzeit," in English "axial age." The pre-Socratic philosophers were influential in Greece, Zoroaster in Persia, Confucius and Laotse in China. In India, the Vedic Period came to its end, the early Upanishads were composed, and

Scroll picture (thangka) of the Buddha.

the notions of karma and reincarnation, very important not only for the oriental cultures, had become highly developed. Communities of ascetics retreated into solitude; the aim of spiritual striving changed from rigid rituals of sacrifice to the searching for the inner essence of the human being and his individual liberation from the cycle of rebirths.

Siddhartha Gautama, son of a noble family, lived his life to the extreme. He was raised surrounded by enjoyments, beauty and luxury and kept away from "real" life with its sometimes ugly, painful experiences. Undertaking four secret excursions to the world outside his palace walls, the young prince met head-on with old age, sickness, and death, and was confronted with human existence being conditioned, which applied to him as well. However, on his fourth excursion he saw a wandering ascetic who had given up all sensual pleasures and was striving for true inner peace. Siddhartha Gautama was deeply impressed by these moving experiences. At the age of 26, the prince left his palace, in the very night his wife gave birth to a son, and he took off to find a path of liberation from the endless cycle of life, death, and rebirth. He became immersed in the doctrines of his time and studied with Vedic scholars. Then he joined a community of ascetics and through their extreme practices ended up on the verge of death.

As legend goes, he stayed alive on just a single grain of rice and a drop of water a day. Eventually he came to the insight that the middle way, which avoids the extremes, is the only path to inner peace, just as the string of a musical instrument only sounds properly if not too tight nor too loose. This path between the extremes, between indulgence and asceticism, between

Subo Das, the young Sadhu, in meditation.

attachment to the worldly and its contemptuous renunciation, is what he found in Bodhgaya. This is where he had settled to meditate beneath a fig tree and where he overcame all inner and outer distractions and eventually became the Awakened One on a full moon night in the month of May.
He kept teaching for forty years. Students would gather around him and follow strict rules of a monks order. As his teachings revoked India's strict caste system and rigid sacrifice rituals, farmers as well as kings counted among his followers. There was no successor of Gautama Buddha, but nevertheless his doctrine rapidly spread to many countries in Asia. At these times, he was actually not the only one searching for new spiritual perspectives. Simultaneously with the Buddha, for example, Mahavira established the Jain religion going far beyond Buddhism in terms of emphasizing the renunciation of the worldly.

Soon after the decease of the Noble One, the Buddhist community split up into different schools, which at the turn of the eras gave rise to Mahayana Buddhism, the Great Vehicle. Contrary to the early schools, the Mahayana did not focus on the liberation and enlightenment of the individual monk, but allowed every practitioner to achieve liberation. Its ideal is the Bodhisattva who strives for enlightenment for the purpose of helping other beings on their paths. This helped pave the way for Buddhism to become a religion for the public. In the Mahayana as well, numerous schools were formed, and when later on Buddhism was influenced by magical tantric teachings, the branch of Vajrayana came up, which has been flourishing until today, especially in Tibetan cultural surroundings.

A Hindu pilgrim in Janakpur, South Nepal.

As different as the doctrines and methods of the various Buddhist schools may be and although the original Buddhist teachings may have been pervaded by countless practices and thoughts of other spiritual paths – some basic points are common to all Buddhist schools. One is, among others, the Noble Eightfold Path, taught by the Buddha as a path to overcome suffering and to achieve awakening and enlightenment:

Right view – the understanding of the doctrine; right resolve – the decision to live according to this understanding and strive to accomplish the path; right speech – to avoid lying, harsh words, useless talk, and slander; right action – to avoid negative actions like killing and stealing; right livelihood – to avoid jobs like butchering, which go against the ethics of the Eightfold Path; right effort – the practice of patience and equanimity and the enhancement of positive actions; right mindfulness – awareness of every single moment of life and its feelings, thoughts, and actions; right concentration – to turn the mind within and concentrate in meditation. A holistic spiritual path consists of these eight steps, which cover the three spheres of wisdom, ethics, and meditation.

The eight chapters of this book go along the Eightfold Path in a very special way. Words of wisdom, not only from Buddhist sources, are tackled or clarified by Dieter Glogowski's photographs. Word and image together are meant to express what is inexpressible, are meant to make inner feelings resound in those who read and observe, to inspire them on their individual spiritual path, and to show the common aims of the various kinds of religious paths.

Franz Binder

Young monks during a peace demonstration in Dharamsala.

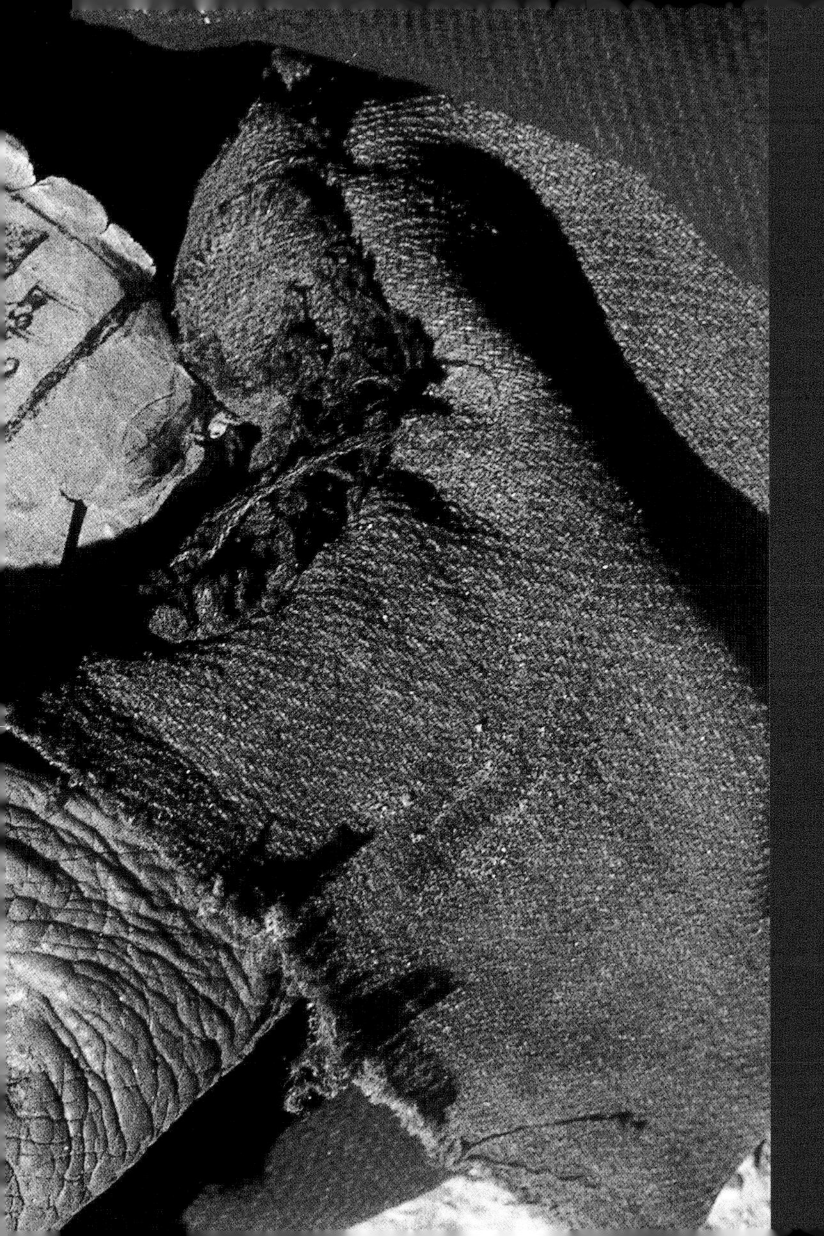

ཡང་དག་པའི་ལྟ་བ།

Wisdom

Wisdom, right insight, the understanding of the doctrine, is inevitable for embarking on the spiritual path. This is why the “Wheel of Dharma” is a basic symbol of all Buddhist schools. In Sarnath, by giving his first ever speech, the Buddha turned the Wheel of Dharma for the first time. Its eight spokes represent the Eightfold Path and the proper application of wisdom. The hub stands for the world’s axis and symbolizes ethical discipline, which stabilizes the mind. The perimeter as the limitation represents concentration, which is inevitable to realize wisdom in one’s meditation.

The path to enlightenment is nothing else but the rediscovery
of our Buddha nature that we have forgotten.
When the wind has blown away the clouds from the sky,
you can see the sun again – actually, it had never stopped shining.

Dilgo Khyentse Rinpoche

Young monks at the giant Maitreya statue at Likir Monastery, Indus valley near Leh, North India.

The first requirement of any spirituality is fearlessness.

For a coward it is impossible to act virtuously.

Mahatma Gandhi

Gandhi statue in front of the Tibetan Ganden Monastery in exile near Hubli, South India.

In this world, hatred is never conquered by hatred. Among human kind, violence is never stopped by counter-violence. Injuries can never be healed by revenge and retaliation. The only way is reconciliation, letting go, and forgiveness.

From the Dhammapada

The future Buddha Maitreya in Tikse Monastery, Leh valley, Ladakh, North India.

Rely on the message of the teacher and not on his personality.

Rely on the meaning of his words and not on the words alone.

Rely on their ultimate meaning and not on the provisional.

Rely on your wisdom mind and not on your ordinary judging mind.

Sogyal Rinpoche

The young monk Tenzing with his 95-year-old teacher Sonam Yospel, Lingshed Monastery, Ladakh, Zanskar.

We should make an effort to develop genuine affection for each other and to clearly realize and acknowledge that we all belong to the same human family. At the same time we have to accept frankly that any world-view and philosophical school could be a means to solve the problems of the human race.

The 14th Dalai Lama

Pilgrim holding a photograph of the Dalai Lama, in the yard of Likir Monastery, Ladakh, North India.

Materially, we are backward, but spiritually, in terms of development of the mind, we are quite rich. We Tibetans are Buddhists and we practice Buddhism in probably its most comprehensive form – including all aspects of the Buddhist teachings, also the tantra – and through our devoted practice we were able to maintain a living tradition.

The 14th Dalai Lama

Tashi and Dolma by the chortens at Dirapuk Gompa, Mt. Kailash, West Tibet.

To develop our patience we need a person – as strange as it may sound – who purposely and repeatedly hurts us. Such people give us the real chance to practice tolerance. They put our inner strength to the test, in a way even our teacher cannot do. Patience protects us from losing our courage.

The 14th Dalai Lama

Mani stone with Om Mani Padme Hum, the Mantra of Avalokiteshvara, the Buddha of compassion.

Who does not search, will not find. The river does not flow toward the people, who may know about it, but do not want to go near. They have to approach, if they wish to scoop up its waters.

Hildegard of Bingen

Hand of a young monk following the text of the Buddha's words in a puja, Ladakh, North India.

Like a child also the wise is someone who can marvel at anything.

Drukpa Rinpoche

Sonam and Tashi, young monks at Lingshed Monastery, Zanskar, North India.

Each time the losses and deceptions of life teach us about impermanence, they bring us closer to the truth. When you fall from a great height, there is only one possible place to land: on the ground, the ground of truth.

And if you have the understanding that comes from spiritual practice, then falling is in no way a disaster but the discovery of an inner refuge.

Sogyal Rinpoche

Tibetan man at the “butter lamp offering place” by the Boudhanath Stupa, Kathmandu, Nepal.

What is the changeless we rediscover at death? The radiance of being, the sun of naturalness. As long as death is not accepted, you remain incomplete, deprived of your deepest nature, of your eternal consciousness. Fear of life and fear of death make happiness impossible.

Drukpa Rinpoche

95-year-old monk Sonam Yospel of Lingshed Monastery passed away in 2006, Zanskar, North India.

At the moment of dying we cannot take anything except the seeds of our life-long efforts, and our mental knowledge.

The 14th Dalai Lama

Old Tibetan lady Dolma Tzering gazing farewell after her grandchildren, Lhasa, Tibet.

Who knows others is intelligent.

Who knows himself is wise.

Who defeats others has energy.

Who defeats himself is strong.

Who is successful has willpower.

Who has modesty is rich.

Who maintains his position has perseverance.

Who does not get lost even at death has life.

Laotse

Two Tibetan nuns circumambulating Mt. Kailash by means of full-length prostration, West Tibet.

It is important to know that there are three kinds of wisdom:

Wisdom resulting from listening,

wisdom resulting from reflection and

wisdom resulting from meditation.

The 14th Dalai Lama

Pilgrim at Lake Manasarovar holding an amulet with a photograph of the Dalai Lama, Tibet.

Suffering is a result of ignorance.

That is why ignorance has to be removed.

Ignorance essentially means grasping at the "ego"

and at the permanence of appearances.

Matthieu Ricard

Tibetan pilgrim woman with her handheld prayer cylinder at the shores of Lake Manasarovar in West Tibet.

Only objects, which you do not desire,

make you rich.

Mahatma Gandhi

Hindu pilgrim on his way to Mt. Kailash, West Tibet.

Enlightened beings know that the world has not to be changed in order to banish all pain, but your heart.

Anthony de Mello

The Brahmin Shiva at his lodging place in Pashupatinath, Kathmandu, Nepal.

Religions are different paths all leading to the same objective.
What does it matter to take different paths,
if eventually we arrive at the same destination?

Mahatma Gandhi

Nepali girl Sina and the Sadhu Hanuman performing a fire offering ritual at Pashupatinath, Nepal.

It is an unquestionable progress to know the form and exact dimensions of the planet Earth.
But whether it is round or flat does not change the meaning of life very much.

Matthieu Ricard

600-year-old prayer cylinder in the legendary city of Lo Mantang, Mustang, Nepal.

Outer peace without inner peace is impossible.

The 14th Dalai Lama

Tibetan monk as well as two nuns performing their morning meditation in Boudhanath, Kathmandu, Nepal.

The Buddha's life story shows us the three sections of the practice path:
first comes ethical discipline, then one-pointed meditation, and then wisdom.
And it also shows us that the path takes time.

The 14th Dalai Lama

Nuns Tsering, Tashi, and Dolma in front of their newly constructed nunnery in Lingshed, Zanskar, North India.

ཡང་དག་པ་འི་ངག

Consciousness

When the conch shell sounds from the roofs of the monasteries in the Himalayas, monks are called to their early morning prayers. The penetrating sound carries far out into the cold, clear air of the high plains and snowy mountains. It stands for the Buddha's voice of teaching, and it resounds fearlessly into all directions to awaken human beings from their sleep of ignorance and to lift them to a consciousness of higher purpose. The awakening of the inner senses, a change of consciousness is the beginning of every spiritual path, which eventually leads to liberation and enlightenment.

To see what is here and now, that is contemplation.

Swami Prajnanpad

Sunrise in the Khumbu area, the land of the Sherpa people, Nepal.

We are what we think.

All we are arises from our thoughts.

With our thoughts we create the world.

From the Dhammapada

Rays of light falling on Gybon-la, a Tibetan praying at Choku Monastery near Mt. Kailash, West Tibet.

As soon as you lose patience, as soon as your intellect is overwhelmed and paralyzed by emotions, your ability of analysis gets lost. However, if you are patient due to your altruistic attitude you will not forfeit your mental powers. On the contrary, you will be able to enhance them and use your analytical abilities to find out how to overcome the negativity you are encountering.

The 14th Dalai Lama

First rays of sun shining on Boudhanath Stupa – monk Tashi Dorje contemplating in view of the pigeons about to be fed, Kathmandu, Nepal.

Tauten your life like the strings of a musical instrument.
Your resolutions should not be too taut lest they break;
they should not be too loose either, or else they will not sound.
Your compassion has to include yourself;
you must learn to feel with yourself and others.

Samyutta Nikaya

Young monk Tzering Gyaltzen on the roof of Sera Monastery in exile, South India.

Mindfulness when speaking,

mastery over the body,

awareness of the ways of the mind;

equanimity in the face of abuse,

never in fury;

this is the path of great progress.

From the Dhammapada

Monks of Sera Monastery in exile holding their daily exercises in debate, South India.

We grow up to create something, to bring something into the world, to accomplish life – and not to destroy, to suppress, to curtail. Willpower, clarity, and love are the three keys to success.

Drukpa Rinpoche

Finishing touches to the mask just before the dance performance at Wangdi Dzong, Bhutan.

Buddhist nuns in the yard of Kopan Monastery, Kathmandu Valley.

We are not independent individuals, but an interdependent multiplicity.
Jack Kornfield

A genuine friendly smile plays an important role in everyday life.

How to bring it about has a lot to do with your attitude.

You cannot expect others to smile at you if you don't smile at them.

Much depends clearly on your own behavior.

The 14th Dalai Lama

Broken plate with the image of the 14th Dalai Lama, found in the hollow of a chorten, Mustang, Nepal.

Good human beings can be recognized from afar, like the peaks of the Himalayan range. This is because human beings who practice compassion and benefit others transform their fellow human beings. In the long run, no one can withdraw from the love and affection of the wise.

From the Dhammapada

Two Tibetan pilgrims circumambulating the Potala Palace by means of full-length prostrations, Lhasa, Tibet.

Learn to grasp the moment! Do not sneak away; do not escape to the delusions of the past or the future. Bring your mind to where you are, with an acute awareness for the present moment. This is where we are. There is no other place than here.

Drukpa Rinpoche

Old Tibetan lady on pilgrimage at Samye Monastery, Central Tibet.

We should work for the benefit of our fellow human beings.
And if in the process we are confronted with suffering,
we will have to tolerate it.
The experience of suffering need not take away our courage,
for there is no experience which, getting used to it,
will not become bearable.

The 14th Dalai Lama

Tibetan pilgrims with an "illegal" photograph of the Dalai Lama – since the decree of the Chinese ten years ago, possession of a Dalai Lama picture has been an offense, Lake Manasarovar, West Tibet.

I have shown you the paths that lead to liberation.
You need to know, however, that liberation depends on yourself.

Buddha Shakyamuni

Monk Tsewang Jorges performing his morning meditation at Shey Gompa, Leh Valley, Ladakh.

Where there is inner strength and self-confidence,

there is no room for mistrust, fear, and doubt.

The 14th Dalai Lama

Young monk from Sera Monastery near Lhasa, Tibet.

The fool who is conscious of his folly

is rightfully considered wise;

but the fool who thinks he has knowing

is truly a fool.

From the Dhammapada

Beggar man offering the traditional Tibetan welcome, Shigatse, Central Tibet.

Education has to be given in accordance with the nature of the child, which is essentially good. The main factor is to raise a child in an atmosphere of love and affection. Even if from a perspective of what would be the best, the human qualities should develop side by side with kindness – if it were necessary to decide upon one, the great common qualities or kindness, then the latter must be chosen.

The 14th Dalai Lama

Young Motup by his parents' field taking a break from harvesting, Lingshed, Ladakh, North India.

The universe is the soul's energy; and from this energy life, consciousness, and the elements originate. The universe is the soul's willpower, and from this willpower the law of cause and effect originates. Out of the soul, oneness became multiplicity; but within the soul, multiplicity is one.

From the Upanishads

Sadhu Ram Baba with his serpent staff, Pashupatinath, Nepal.

The mental exists in a vicious circle.

It creates problems for itself and then tries to solve them.

Swami Prajnanpad

Morning atmosphere at a bathing pond in Janakpur, South Nepal.

Erroneously, man has identified with an imaginary soul, or ego.

If he transfers his feeling of identity on his true being, the immortal soul,

he will discover that all pain is unreal.

He will not even be able to imagine the state of suffering anymore.

Paramahansa Yogananda

Sadhu Hanuman in Pashupatinath, Nepal.

A serpent regularly sheds its skin; similarly we too have to abandon a lot of past prejudice all the time. We have to let go of wrong attitudes and desires. Our lives are characterized by change and transformation; we have to adapt to new situations constantly. This is how we get to know freedom and the happiness of life.

Digha Nikaya

Sleeping Vishnu on his bed of serpents in Budhanilkantha, Kathmandu Valley, Nepal.

Freedom is a state of mind – not the freedom from something.

Krishnamurti

Sadhu Muni Baba with his two-meter-long hair, Santabar, South Nepal

Our task is not to increase property, but to be.

Rabindranath Tagore

Female sadhvi Muka Das, Nepal.

Compassion

The waters of immortality flowing from this treasure vase are an auspicious never ceasing stream of long life, wealth, and affluence. However, the limitless quantities of life elixir contained in this vase are not confined to impermanent worldly treasures for earthly existence, but mainly consist of mental riches. These are the most precious because they lead to liberation, to the end of suffering, to enlightenment, and to true immortality. One of the most precious of these gems is compassion, the main virtue of any spiritual path.

The real essence of human existence is kindness.
There are other qualities that are brought about through education and knowledge,
but if you truly wish to become a human being and to make existence meaningful,
then it is essential to have a good heart.

The 14th Dalai Lama

Children of Tangbe village in the upper Mustang area, Nepal.

Always try to act in a way that people are happy to have met you.

Mother Teresa

Pilgrim boy at the gates of Langbona Monastery at Lake Manasarovar.

I will always be close to those who have trust, and even to those who have no trust, although they do not see me. My compassion will protect my children for ever and ever.

Padmasambhava

Little Dolma with her father's yaks circumambulating Mt. Kailash, West Tibet.

Friendliness and gentleness open up hearts.

Vincent de Paul

Young monks with the image of the 17th Karmapa in the yard of Rumtek Monastery, Sikkim.

We must keep in mind the happiness of others, not our own.
Most of all, we should wish well especially to those we consider our enemies
who are ill-treating us. What else should possibly be the meaning of compassion?

Dilgo Khyentse Rinpoche

Little Tibetan pilgrim boy Norbu at the Jokhang in Lhasa, Tibet.

In one respect we are all the same, our friends, our enemies,
all living beings and ourselves:
We want to be happy and we do not want to suffer.
In this respect we are all the same.

The 14th Dalai Lama

Two nomad girls on the Tibetan high plateau desert, the Changtang.

To develop a kind heart is not only appropriate for all those who follow a religion, but for everyone who considers himself a member of the human family.

The 14th Dalai Lama

Stupa or chorten, three-dimensional symbolic mandala in the middle of Bhutan.

Great compassion is like a wish-fulfilling jewel.

It fulfills one's own hopes and those of others.

Shabkar

Ancient milk-powder tin transformed into a prayer cylinder – nevertheless filled with rice paper rolls 100,000-fold inscribed with the mantra of compassion, Upper Pisang, Nepal.

光明牌全脂奶粉
Bright
WHOLE MILK POWDER

No matter how many sacred words you read,
no matter how many you recite –
what value do they have for you
if you do not act accordingly?

From the Dhammapada

Prayer-flag pole at the west side of Mt. Kailash, West Tibet.

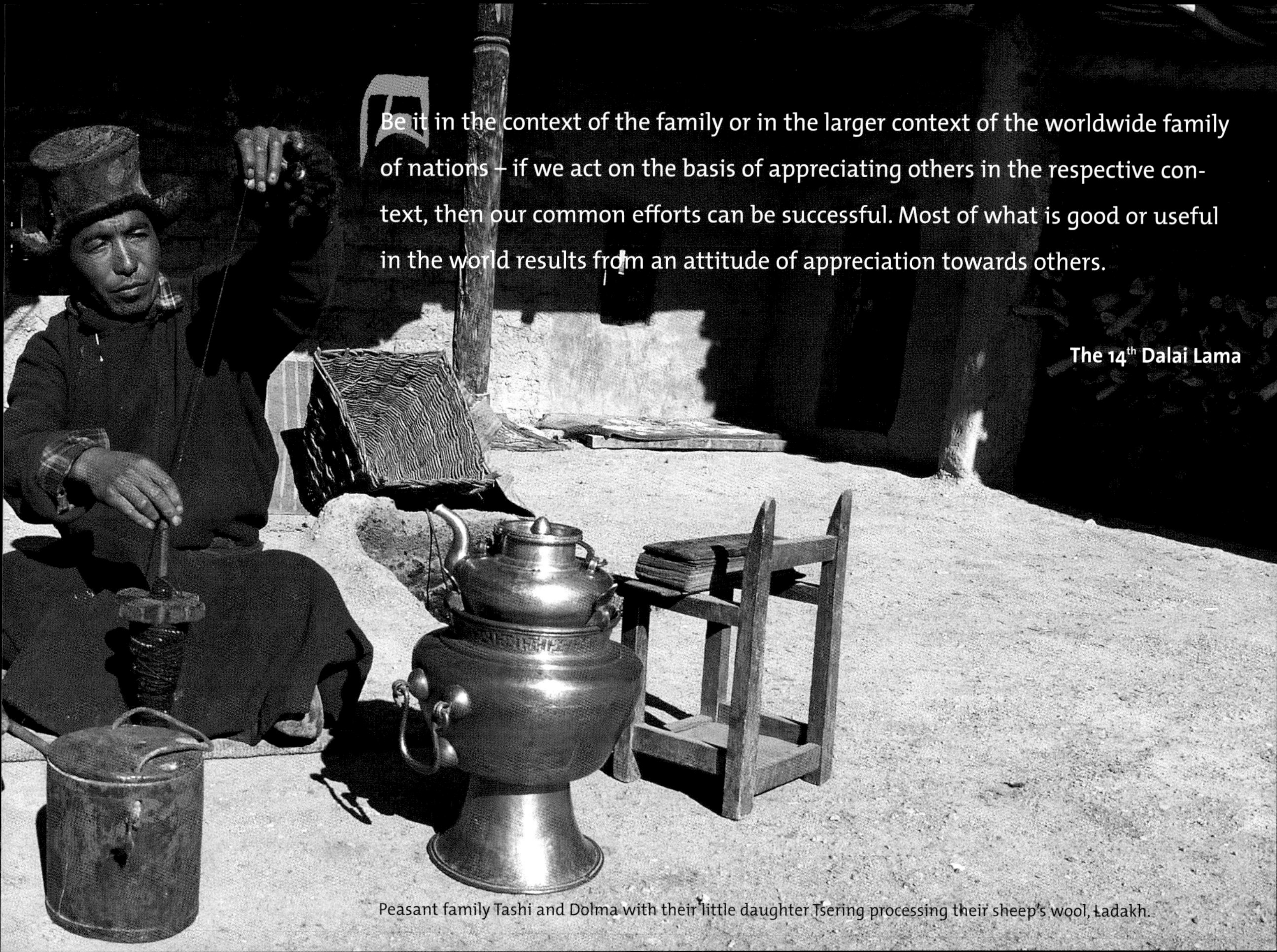

Be it in the context of the family or in the larger context of the worldwide family of nations – if we act on the basis of appreciating others in the respective context, then our common efforts can be successful. Most of what is good or useful in the world results from an attitude of appreciation towards others.

The 14th Dalai Lama

Peasant family Tashi and Dolma with their little daughter Tsering processing their sheep's wool, Ladakh.

Compassion is the practical approach
and wisdom the philosophical view
to understanding reality.

The 14th Dalai Lama

Indian beggar in Dharamsala – visitors leaving the precincts of the Dalai Lama's monastery following a four-hour teaching session, North India.

The intelligence of love and compassion alone
can solve the problems of life.

Krishnamurti

Rai Kumar is in tears mourning for his deceased mother, Pashupatinath, Nepal.

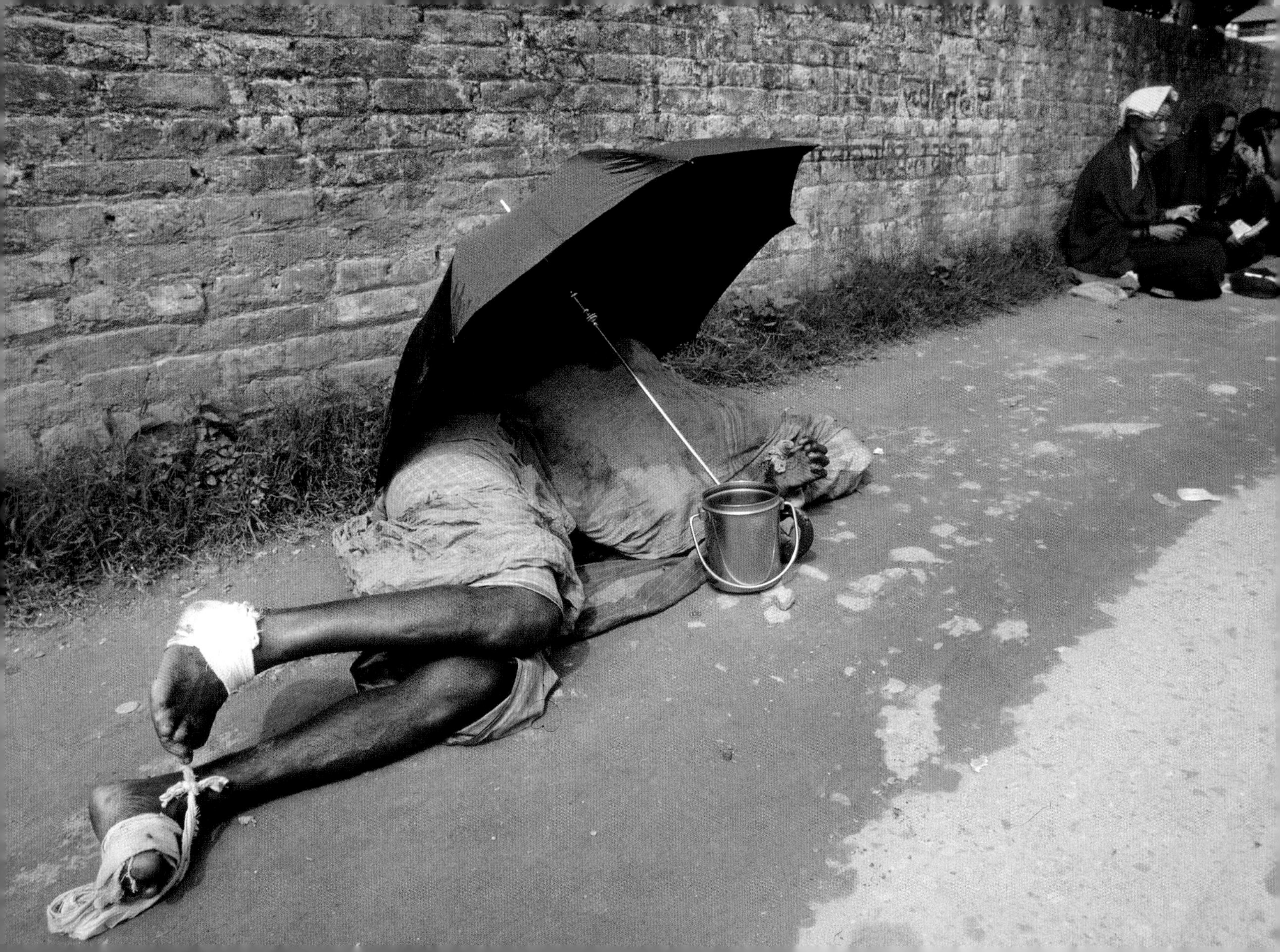

One powerful way to evoke compassion is to think of others as exactly the same as you. "After all," the Dalai Lama explains, "all human beings are the same – made of human flesh, bones, and blood. We all want happiness and want to avoid suffering. Further, we have an equal right to be happy. In other words, it is important to realize our sameness as human beings."

Sogyal Rinpoche

Dying leper and praying monk in the streets of Kathmandu, Nepal.

There is no life without pain.

But it is in your hands

if pain makes you suffer or grow.

Matthias Stöbener

Man sitting at the entrance of Swayambunath Stupa with his artificial legs unstrapped, Kathmandu, Nepal.

The heart is like a garden.

It can grow compassion or fear, ill will or love.

What kind of seedlings would you like to grow there?

Jack Kornfield

Scottish pilgrim Yajanang Das has been roaming about the Himalayas for 25 years as a disciple of Krishna, Pashupatinath, Nepal.

Sadhus in Pashupatinath, Kathmandu, Nepal.

The only way to attain lasting peace is mutual trust, respect, love, and compassion. This is the only way!

The 14th Dalai Lama

CHINA'S RECORD IN TIBET

MORE THAN A MILLION KILLED
MORE THAN 6,000 MONASTERIES
DESTROYED THOUSANDS IN
PRISON HUNDREDS STILL MISSING

'NO MATTER HOW HARD THE WIND OF EVIL MAY BLOW, IT CAN NEVER EXTINGUISH THE FLAME OF TRUTH' HIS HOLINESS THE XIV DALAI LAMA

CHINA, GET
OUT OF TIBET

www.friendsoftibet.org

CHINA'S RECORD IN TIBET

MORE THAN A MILLION KILLED
MORE THAN 6,000 MONASTERIES
DESTROYED THOUSANDS IN
PRISON HUNDREDS STILL MISSING

'NO MATTER HOW HARD THE WIND OF EVIL MAY BLOW, IT CAN NEVER EXTINGUISH THE FLAME OF TRUTH' HIS HOLINESS THE XIV DALAI LAMA

CHINA, GET
OUT OF TIBET

www.friendsoftibet.org

We are not angry with the stick that hits, but with the person who strikes the blow;
this person on his part, however, acts under the power of hatred.
That is why it is hatred that we should hate.

Shantideva

Poster in Dharamsala, North India.

free tibet !

Nonviolence is the greatest power that human beings have at their command.
It is more powerful than the most powerful lethal weapons,
which the wealth of human creativity may have invented.

Mahatma Gandhi

Tibetan monk reciting his mantras in the yard of the Great Stupa of Boudhanath, Kathmandu, Nepal.

SAVE TIBET
FOR
WORLD PEACE
FREE TIBET
HELP END THE CHINESE OCCUPATION

When we investigate our long history of hatred and fury, we realize the obvious necessity to find better solutions. We can solve our problems by peaceful means only – peaceful words alone are not enough, but we need a peaceful mind and a peaceful heart, too. This way we will accomplish a better world.

The 14th Dalai Lama

Posted at a wall in Dharamsala, North India.

After all, every religion serves the purpose to make us better human beings: human beings who are more tolerant, more compassionate, and less egoistic.

The 14th Dalai Lama

The Bhutanese nun Nenchen meditating the offering of a mandala, Paro, Bhutan.

In the deepest sense we really are sisters and brothers. Therefore we must share our individual sufferings with each other. Mutual concern, trust, and interest in the wellbeing of others are our greatest hopes for lasting world peace.

The 14th Dalai Lama

Peace demonstration of monks in Dharamsala, North India.

ཡང་དག་པའི་རྩོལ་བ།

Equanimity

The serene equanimity of a victorious one, who has conquered the world of phenomena and desires – this is what is expressed by the round victory banners that decorate the temples and roofs of Tibetan monasteries. Once carried into battle by victorious soldiers, in Buddhism today they symbolize the victory of knowledge over ignorance, the triumph over all forms of anger and hatred, the overcoming of death, suffering, and of all obstacles. They are symbols of liberation and signs of the mind's ultimate victory, a victory that cannot be gained through worldly arms, but only through wisdom and equanimity.

Kindness and goodwill is the key to peace and harmony in family life.

Families must educate and train their children.

Parents should be the foremost mental and spiritual teachers of their children.

The 14th Dalai Lama

Peasant women on their barley field in Pidmu village, Zanskar, North India.

Karma is neither fatalistic nor deterministic. Karma is our ability to be creative and to bring about change; it means that we can decide how and why we act. We can change ourselves. The future is in our own hands. The Buddha says:

Karma is creative like an artist,
karma expresses itself like a dancer.

Buddhist wisdom

Jesters at the festival of mask dancing at Wangdi Dzong, Bhutan.

Conflict or warfare can be settled, but further conflict and warfare will arise if the mental attitude of human beings does not change. Is there not any means to find inner peace, which does not depend on health, power, success, money, and sense pleasures, – inner peace, which is the source of outer peace?

Matthieu Ricard

Bhutanese jesters making fun of two policemen at the monastery festival of Wangdi Dzong, Bhutan.

If people laugh they are able to think!

The 14th Dalai Lama

Bhutanese man laughingly waving his felt cap at the photographer; it is rolled up to look like a penis, a symbol supposed to expel demons.

The purpose of making money should be the happiness of people, and not the other way round.

The 14th Dalai Lama

Monsoon time at the Nepalese-Tibetan border – minstrel at the roadside.

What we have done in our lifetime makes us what we are at the time of death. And everything counts, really everything.

Buddhist wisdom

Door chorten leading toward Tangbe village, Mustang, Nepal.

Man alone has the power to destroy the Earth.

Birds or rabbits could not do that.

But if man has the power to destroy the Earth,

he also has the power to save it from destruction.

The 14th Dalai Lama

Winter scenery upon reaching Khumjung in the Khumbu area, Nepal.

For me it is obvious that material progress alone cannot replace the traditional spiritual or humanitarian values, which have been responsible for the development of the world's culture, as we know it today. In my opinion we should try to reach a balance between material and spiritual increase.

The 14th Dalai Lama

Peasants and monks from Lingshed transporting timber, Ladakh, North India.

Every gambler has to accept the cards
that life deals out to him or her.
But as soon as the respective persons have them in their hands,
they alone have to decide how to play them out
in order to win the game.

Palu Rinpoche

It is four years since the volleyball D-juniors of Pidmu have been proud owners of a volleyball, but unfortunately for three years now, it cannot be inflated anymore because the bladder inside is broken.

Those who have realized the doctrine

and are never upset by anything are in peace wherever

they go, and for them that is ultimate happiness.

Sutta-Nipata

Ladakhi peasant with a photograph of the 14th Dalai Lama and a mala in his hands in the yard of Lingshed Monastery, Ladakh.

The destination of your life's journey is nothing you could not reach:

it is the coming home to yourself.

Every moment you spend in perfect accord with yourself

is a step toward this destination.

Matthias Stöbener

Tiger Nest Monastery hanging precipitously and looking unreal in a 400-meter-high (1,300 FT) wall of granite, Bhutan.

When you are calm and relaxed, you are not even perturbed by your enemy.

The 14th Dalai Lama

Old peasant in Bhutan.

We exchange the breath of air with the rain forests. We drink the very water that flows into the ocean. Water and air are integral parts of our lives. And we are part of the whole world. We realize that we depend on each other, that we are related to each other. Then we will deal with all of nature carefully, we are part of it.

From the Suttanipada

School children protecting themselves from the monsoon rain with a banana leaf, Nepal.

Tibetan herdswoman Dolma milking goats on the Changtang, East Ladakh, India.

We want more and more and more. This is, in a certain sense, true poverty –
being hungry and hungry and hungry all the time, without a little time of contentment.

The 14th Dalai Lama

Little monk Sonam Tashi with his toy car, homemade from wire, Rizong Monastery, Ladakh.

Our inner life radiates outside.

Ayya Khema

Because of his immeasurable goodness, his compassion, and his loving smile, Lama Sandup from Lingshed Monastery is a living example for all the valley inhabitants, North India.

Every creature is connected to another, and every being is held by another.

Hildegard of Bingen

Young monks at Punakha Dzong, Bhutan.

Nobody hopes for the worse. Therefore happiness is the true goal in life: to gain happier days, happier weeks, happier years, and a happier human community. As the mental attitude is a main factor, in my opinion we should pay more attention to our inner development.

The 14th Dalai Lama

Young monks with their teachers on the roof of their monastery in Dharamsala, North India.

Be open, simple, less self-concerned, and have fewer desires.

Laotse

Monks from Lingshed Monastery, Ladakh.

You are your own lord and master. Your future depends on yourself.

Nobody else can take the future of your life into his hands;

the present life can only be shouldered by yourself.

Buddha Shakyamuni

A Tibetan from Kham on the way to his village in Dolpo.

Touch all living beings around you

like the heavenly mother of the world does.

Treat all beings as if they were your children.

Do not harm any other living being,

because they feel like you feel.

They are your brothers and sisters.

Learn to let go of the things around you in good time.

That is the key to ultimate bliss.

From the Digha Nikaya

Nepali school boy Susan with his flute, Kathmandu, Nepal.

The very moment man increases his daily wishes, he fails to follow his ideal of supreme thinking and living fully. True happiness of man lies in contentment.

Mahatma Gandhi

Saintly pilgrim Rade Baba at a Shiva Lingam in Gosaikunde, North Nepal.

ॐ नमः शिवाय

ཡང་དག་པའི་འཚོ་བ།

Love

Fearlessly and without hindrance, like a fish swimming in the water, a human being freely moves around in the ocean of suffering – a human being who has attained the state of liberation and enlightenment, who has realized love for all living beings in his heart. He cannot be drowned in the currents of obstacles and temptations of the cycle of death and rebirth; after all, life is limited, but love is immeasurable. Therefore the two fishes of this auspicious symbol do not only stand for love and fulfillment in marriage, like in China, but also for spiritual liberation, like for Hindus, Buddhists, and Jains.

It is very difficult to gain peace and harmony through competition or hatred. To practice kindness is therefore very, very important and immensely precious for the human society.

The 14th Dalai Lama

Young monks of Lingshed Monastery, Ladakh.

There is a secret of love. Those who love experience the stars' power of attraction, the fire of suns, the beginning and the end of worlds. They die and are reborn in the same body.

Drukpa Rinpoche

Tibetan nomad woman with her two children on the kora (circumambulation) of Mt. Kailash, West Tibet.

Don’t look for perfection in a world of change.

Instead make your love perfect.

Jack Kornfield

Peasant woman Susmita with her little son in front of a symbol of protection painted on the wall of her barn in the Terai, South Nepal.

Perfect love chases away our fears, because it has no wishes, no demands; it does not bargain, it does not judge and has no negative apprehensions. Love is simple, it is present, and it acts.

Anthony de Mello

With his sick mother on his back, young peasant Madenra is on a pilgrimage to the holy place of Muktinath in the Annapurna region, Nepal.

Peace springs from those who sow love and then leave it to transform into action. We are born to love and to be loved.

Mother Teresa

At the holy lakes of Gosaikunde in the morning of the full moon festival, North Nepal.

When you instinctively react from your heart to the joys and sufferings of other human beings, then you know that you have lost your self and that you have realized oneness with the human race. Then, at last, love has come.

Anthony de Mello

Peasant carrying his sick wife on his back and begging for alms at the Buddhist Boudhanath Stupa, Nepal.

Bhandar
DEVPATTAN, KTM-

The great religions of this world, be it Buddhism, Judaism, Christianity, Islam, Confucianism, Hinduism, Jainism, Sikhism, Taoism, or Zoroastrianism – they all have similar concepts of the ideal of love. The ultimate meaning of their religious and spiritual practice is charity in action.

The 14th Dalai Lama

Three Hindu pilgrim women on their way to the Shiva Ratri festival in Pashupatinath, Kathmandu, Nepal.

It is vital to leave a lot of room for change in one's relations to another person. Change comes about in times of transition, allowing love actually to ripen and expand. Then one is able to really know the other one – to see him as he is, with his faults and weaknesses, a human being like oneself. Only at this stage one is ready to genuinely commit oneself to the other person – a true act of love.

The 14th Dalai Lama

Three Tibetan women on pilgrimage at the west side of Mt. Kailash during Saga Dawa festival, West Tibet.

We are free to choose if we want to love or to hate.

The 14th Dalai Lama

Young monks Dawa and Norbu in front of a bold relief wall in Sikkim.

ཨོཾམཎིཔདྨེཧཱུྃ

Love is the wish that all sentient beings may enjoy happiness and that they may never be completely separated from happiness. With the power of meditation on love, the Buddha defeated hosts of demons. Thus meditation on love is the supreme protection from evil. By means of meditation we get familiar with love.

The 14th Dalai Lama

Monk Dawa on kora around Shigatse Monastery, praying near a rock painting of the Green Tara, Tibet.

Do not condemn yourself.

Without compassion for ourselves we will not be able to love the world.

Buddha Shakyamuni

Peasant of the Terai in Nepal.

Joy does not arise from wealth and possessions. True joy of life arises from a wise and caring heart. The more of our life force we devote to others, the more of it comes back to us.

From the Sutta Nipata

Brahmin Sutra doing his evening prayers, Pashupatinath, Nepal.

A flower needs sun to become a flower.

A human being needs love to become a human being.

Phil Bosmans

Little Palden in his mother's baby sling on the way to Leh, a four-days walk, Ladakh, North India.

A moment of love makes you patient.

A moment of patience makes you love.

Matthias Stöbener

Ladakhi peasant woman Dolma showing her son Rigzin an ear of barley, Ladakh, North India.

Love makes someone's heart melt into somebody else's heart,

and feel what he feels.

Vincent de Paul

Cozily wrapped in sheepskin by his mother, ten-month-old Tashi is experiencing his first pilgrimage to Mt. Kailash, West Tibet.

Love does not give anything but itself,

and it does not take anything but from itself.

Love does not possess nor does it want to be possessed.

For love is sufficient within love itself.

Khalil Gibran

Lovingly the little child's mother has fixed Kauri shells to its cap for the little soul to hide from the attacks of demons, Lingshed.

Be happy now!

There is no other place for love.

Mahatma Gandhi

Spring festival fire offering in Bhaktapur, Nepal.

Who listens to the soul's music

will master the melody of life.

Swami Sivananda

A Sadhu in Kathmandu Valley, Nepal.

Whatever you do should be determined by love.

Corinthians 1/16, 14

Young girl in Bhutan.

Darkness cannot be dispelled by darkness, only by light.

Hatred cannot be healed by hatred, only by love.

Phil Bosmans

Children playing in the alleyways of the old Kagbeni caravansary, Lower Mustang area, Nepal.

God is a God of the present. He will accept and receive you the way he finds you, not as what you have been, but just as what you are now.

Master Eckehart

Sleeping, well-protected in the monastery yard of Punakha Dzong, Bhutan.

LOVE

ཡང་དག་པའི་ལས་ཀྱི་མཐའ

Transformation

Everything throughout the universe is connected to each other. The nature of reality manifests as a fine net of unceasing transformation within duality – it manifests as a result of death and rebirth, of cause and effect, and, at the same time, as the unity of wisdom and compassion, and of emptiness and dependent origination. The eternal knot, a symbol well known in many world traditions, is irresolvably intertwined in itself without beginning or end. It demonstrates man's link to his karma, the result of his own action; it is a token of love and happiness, and a symbol of the limitless wisdom of the Buddha.

Because in our culture we overvalue the intellect, one would imagine that to become enlightened demands extraordinary intelligence. In fact, many kinds of ingenuity are just further obscurations. There is a Tibetan saying that goes, “If you are too clever, you could miss the point entirely.”

Sogyal Rinpoche

Within sight of Lingshed Monastery, Monk Zapel playing with his cell phone made in India, even though there is no reception in this far off mountainous area.

instax 200
FUJINON LENS

Life is like a river. It does not give itself away at first glance, but if you have a closer look with eyes that finally have widened through the power of the strong desire to see, you will realize that everything is in the process of change in any moment.

Drukpa Rinpoche

Tibetan pilgrim with a Polaroid camera made in China, during Saga Dawa Festival at Mt. Kailash, West Tibet.

BOY
DIJIN BOY

Do not get attached to what is pleasant and joyful.

Do not get attached to suffering and depression, too.

Instead, learn to let go of either in due time.

Do not get chained to beauty like a slave.

Do not get chained to suffering, too.

Everything is in change; either is impermanent.

From the Dhammapada

Tibetan youth at the Chinese mountain biker's monument in Shigatse, Tibet.

In the beginner's mind there are many possibilities,
in the expert's mind there are few.

Shunryu Suzuki

Young monk playing with his Game Boy at Ganden Monastery near Lhasa, Tibet.

Ammonites – fossils from the bottom of the ocean – can be found all over the Himalayas, Lo Mantang, Nepal.

西藏旅游 促进经济繁荣
拉萨市旅游局

A beautiful country is a dream-like illusion,

it is meaningless to get attached to it.

As long as the inner forces of negative emotions are not subdued,

the fight against the outer enemy will never end!

Dilgo Khyentse Rinpoche

Elderly Tibetan lady performing her morning prayers in front of the Potala Palace hung with Chinese slogans, Lhasa, Tibet.

发展西藏旅
促进经济繁荣

It is not the other one who must change, but oneself.

Swami Prajnanpad

A father taking a photograph of his children posing in front of a Chinese jet fighter at the Potala in Lhasa, Tibet.

Life is not like an artificial waterway,

it is not restricted to flow within prescribed boundaries.

Rabindranath Tagore

Poster of London at a Bhutanese market.

LONDON
FAIRSTAR

EXCELLENT

In a world of change and transformation there is no perfection.

Everything is in the process of becoming; no fellow human being is perfect.

If we can realize that, we will not ask too much of anybody.

Buddha Shakyamuni, from the Udana

Butter lamps of the new electrical kind at a market in Lhasa, Tibet.

Great changes take place in small steps.

Lay down one stone every day, never neglecting the site, and the building will grow.

Resist doubt and laziness. Keep your mind awake.

Observe, realize, and love!

Drukpa Rinpoche

Wood carving of a Green Tara at a school in Bhutan.

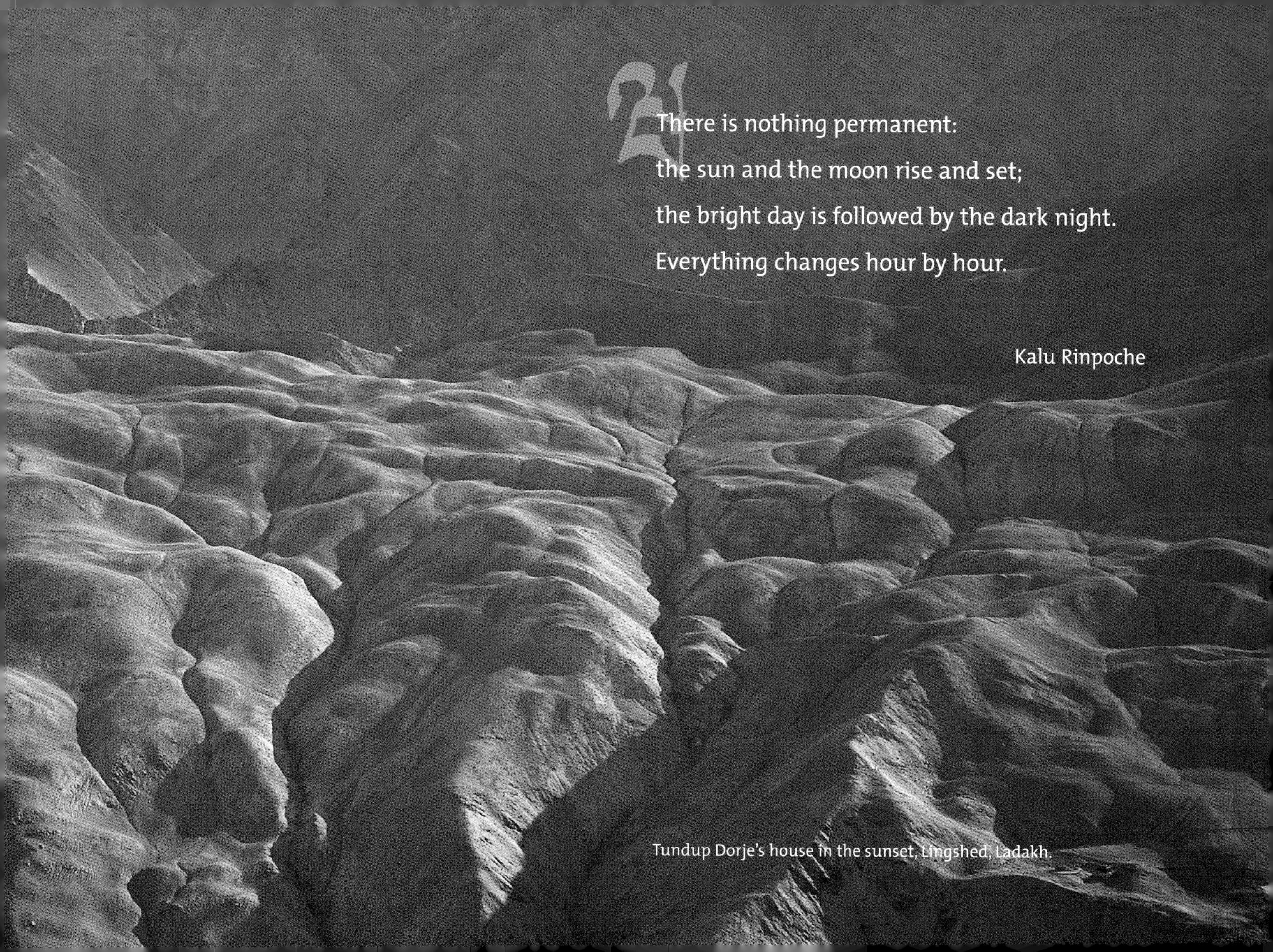

There is nothing permanent:
the sun and the moon rise and set;
the bright day is followed by the dark night.
Everything changes hour by hour.

Kalu Rinpoche

Tundup Dorje's house in the sunset, Lingshed, Ladakh.

In the past, we were thankful that the trees were helping us. Their flowers were our decoration, their fruits were our nourishment, their leaves and fibers were our clothes and gave us shelter. We found refuge in their branches that protected us from wild animals. Their wood kept us warm; we used it for sticks to lean on in old age, or to defend ourselves. We were intimately connected with the trees. Today, as we are surrounded by complicated machines and by computers in our offices, it is easy to lose our connection with nature.

The 14th Dalai Lama

View of barley fields at Stonde, Zanskar, North India.

Time does not stop nor does it wait, but keeps flowing without obstruction.
In the same way our lives are moving on and on. If in our life we experience failure or if an accident occurs, we cannot turn backward, stop the time, and start again.
Looking at it this way, there is no real second chance or possibility.

The 14th Dalai Lama

Mani stone smeared with mineral water advertising, Mustang area, Nepal.

Everything is in the process of change this very moment.
You, too, are involved in unceasing transformation and gradual decay,
and the whole universe with you.

Mark Aurel

Butter tea and Coca Cola, in a field in Ladakh, North India.

always
Coca-Cola
Trademark Regd.
always
Trademark Regd.

SAVE
TIBE

It is my firm conviction that the power of the gun barrel is of limited time.

But the power of truth will increase more and more with time.

The 14th Dalai Lama

Tibetan nun in exile in a Tibetan settlement in Delhi, India.

Everything has its moment.

If the time is not right and, no matter what, you keep trying to have it your way, you will end up in difficulties.

Therefore it is essential to know the moment which is right and which is wrong.

From the One Hundred Parable Sutra

Father and son in their small caravansary on the Western high plains of Tibet.

紅太陽
紅日東升山河壯
東風浩蕩氣象新

What is necessary is not a uniform religion, but mutual respect and tolerance among the followers of the different religions. What we aim at is not bleak consolidation, but unity within the diverse. Any attempt to suffocate traditions, which have originated from common heritage and which have been conditioned by climate and environment, is not only doomed to failure, it is a sacrilege.

Mahatma Gandhi

Hindu festival in Bhaktapur, Nepal.

Over-consumption and wastage of goods, or excessive effort to make money, all of this is not good. By the same token, mere contentment should not be endorsed. Basically, contentment is something to aim at, but frugal living for the sake of it prevents development, and it is deathlike living.

The 14th Dalai Lama

Indian posters in a small shop on the Annapurna trek, West Nepal.

PREITY
things that will
not do them.
God

GOLDEN

And do not forget: your mind is a maze. Follow it thought by thought, notion by notion, dream by dream. Nothing remains as it was. Today you are here, tomorrow there. Today you are looking for something, tomorrow you will find it, and the day after tomorrow you will have lost it again. Happiness and misery, real and unreal are nothing but time passing by. But what is time?

Wolfgang Wenger

Sadhu Ram Das with his traditional harmonium, Pashupatinath, Nepal.

Our life is full of failure and loss. Let us learn in time to let go of things we are attached to. Then we will understand the change that we are exposed to. Let us use such times to transform any situation into something good. Let us do our activities without haste, but with inner peace.

From the Digha Nikaya

Sadhu Ram Das half a year later: he has exchanged his old traditional harmonium with a Chinese synthesizer, Kathmandu, Nepal.

Everything is subject to change and transformation. Our lives are a permanent sequence of different situations and emotions. One situation is coming, the other one is going. Nothing is permanent, nothing is immovable. We should not cling to a certain situation of our consciousness, we should not be attached to a certain image of self.

Milindapana

In honor of his God Shiva, Sadhu Krishna Das has rubbed his body with white ashes, Pashupatinath, Nepal.

21

The more we are able to inwardly disengage from greed,

the more richly we will be given.

Matthias Stöbener

Sadhu teacher Hanuman Baba on pilgrimage with his students Subo Das and Pulto Das, Kali Gandaki Canyon, West Nepal.

ཡང་དག་པའི་དྲན་པ།

Mindfulness

The lotus flower is rooted in mud and grows up in water before it comes to the surface and opens its immaculate blossom towards the sun. Thus it represents the spiritual path of a person, leading from the delusions of deep materialism through the dim ocean of samsara, the experience of cyclic existences, up to the pure radiance of enlightenment; it symbolizes complete purification of body, speech, and mind. Whereas the lotus bud is said to be symbolic for the potential of liberation, which is inherent in every being, the fully blossoming flower expresses complete realization of enlightenment.

It is a great benefit of mindfulness, if we practice it, that we can easily realize whenever the purpose of our action is no longer in accordance with our intentions. Quickly and quietly, we can then readjust.

Matthias Stöbener

The world's largest scroll painting (thangka) is displayed on the occasion of the 15th day of the Tibetan New Year festival (losar) near Sera Monastery, South India.

The practice of mindfulness is nothing else but the practice of loving kindness.

Thich Nhat Hanh

Nylam, Master of Ceremonies, strictly watching over the exact performance of the mask dances, Spituk Monastery, Ladakh.

Recover the innocence of the moment, the simple clarity of things.

Learn to live eternity.

Drukpa Rinpoche

Buddhist monk from Sri Lanka visiting Boudhanath Stupa, Kathmandu, Nepal.

You should develop the capability of joy.

Then you can approach your duties with joy and delight.

You could act like a child playing.

However, when you are tired and exhausted, then it is important to relax.

The 14th Dalai Lama

A smile for the photographer during an 8-hour lecture at Kopan Monastery, Kathmandu, Nepal.

Mindfulness arises from a well-developed consciousness of your own physical and verbal actions, a consciousness, which extends to the world of dreams also. If you pay close attention to your behavior while eating, coming and going, standing and sitting, and so on, then the conditions for mindfulness can put down strong roots.

The 14th Dalai Lama

Constant slight swinging transforms the milk inside the goatskin bladder into butter, Changtang, North Tibet.

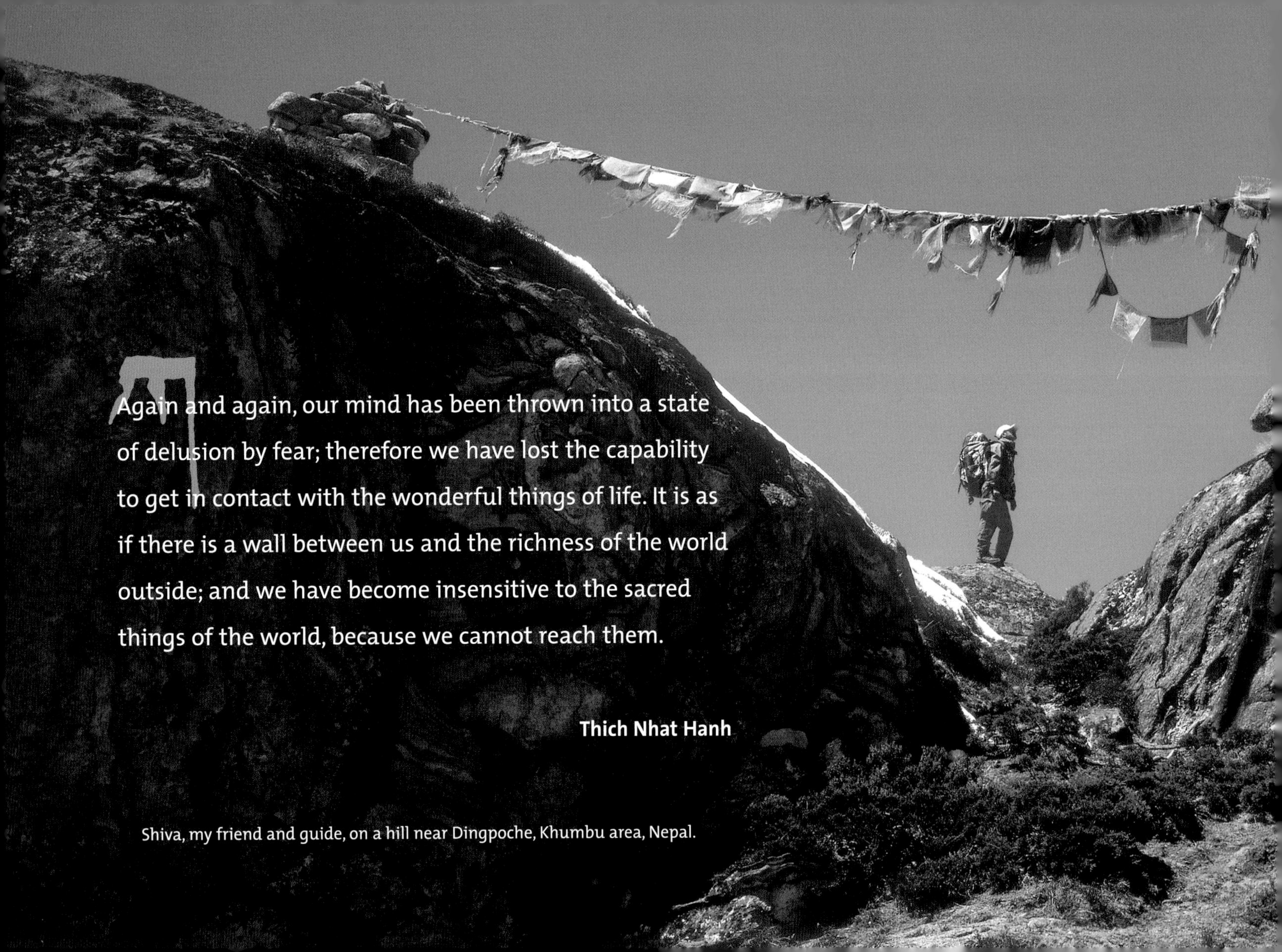

Again and again, our mind has been thrown into a state of delusion by fear; therefore we have lost the capability to get in contact with the wonderful things of life. It is as if there is a wall between us and the richness of the world outside; and we have become insensitive to the sacred things of the world, because we cannot reach them.

Thich Nhat Hanh

Shiva, my friend and guide, on a hill near Dingpoche, Khumbu area, Nepal.

If you live mindfully, you will touch upon what is refreshing, healing and enjoyable. The sources of the positive remain closed for the one who is not mindful.

Matthias Stöbener

Monk Tupchen of Gyangdrag Monastery at Mt. Kailash beholding a Buddha statue, West Tibet.

Take your time to be happy.

Time is not a highway from the cradle to the grave,

but a parking-lot in the sun.

Phil Bosmans

Making of a clay mask in a Bhutanese art school.

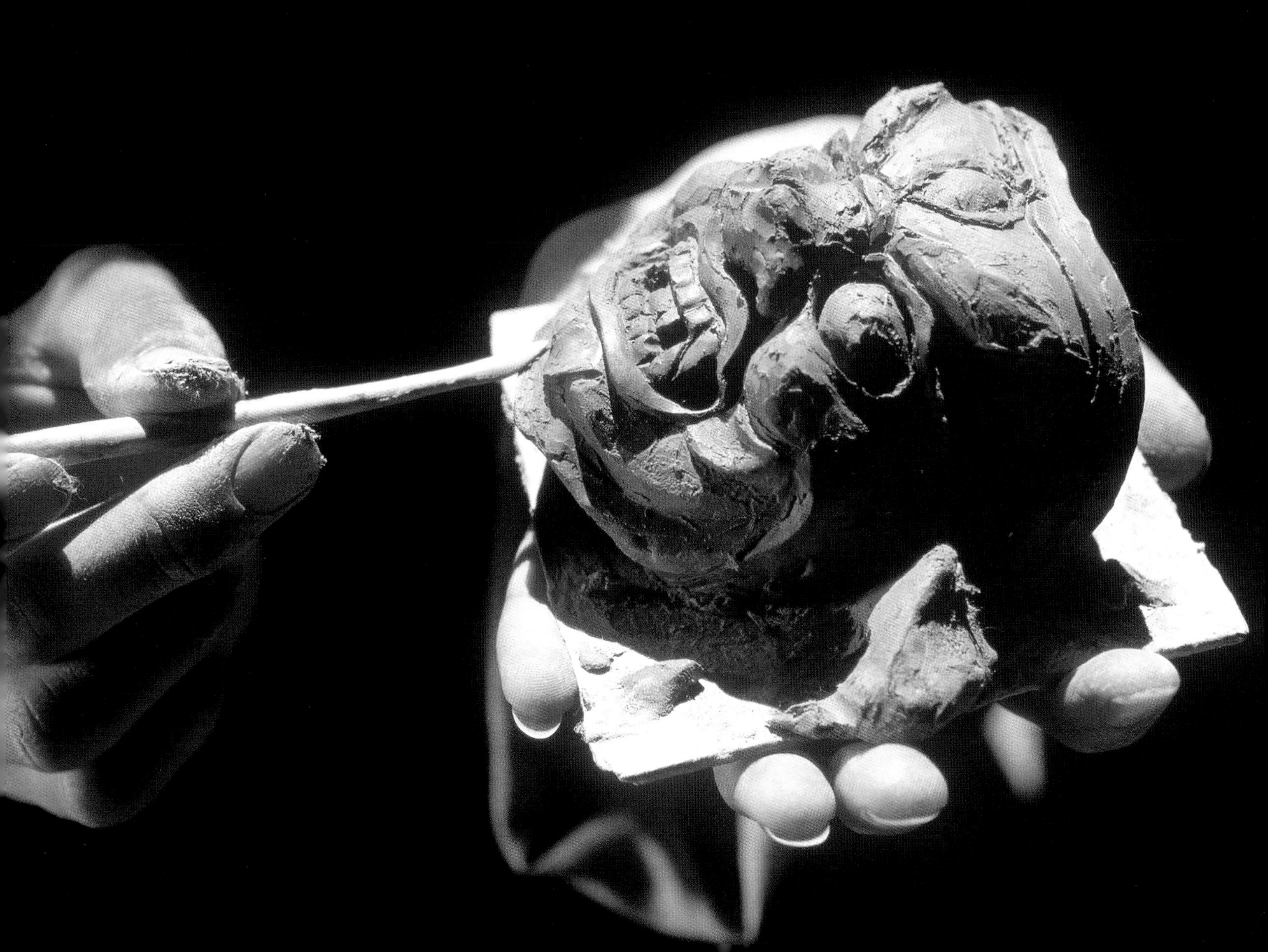

To be present means to let go of the primacy of thinking
and to come back to your senses, in the true meaning of the word;
not to abstract anymore, but to experience.

Anthony de Mello

Tibetan thangka painting school in the Norbulingka temple near Dharamsala, North India.

Your everyday life is your temple and your religion.

Khalil Gibran

Monks Pema and Sandup in Dharamsala, North India.

MAY
PEACE
PREVAIL
ON
EARTH

Real life is experienced here and now.

The past has already gone; the future has not yet come.

Only in the present moment can we truly touch life.

Thich Nhat Hanh

Tibetan pilgrim woman at the Kumbum chorten in Gyantse, Tibet.

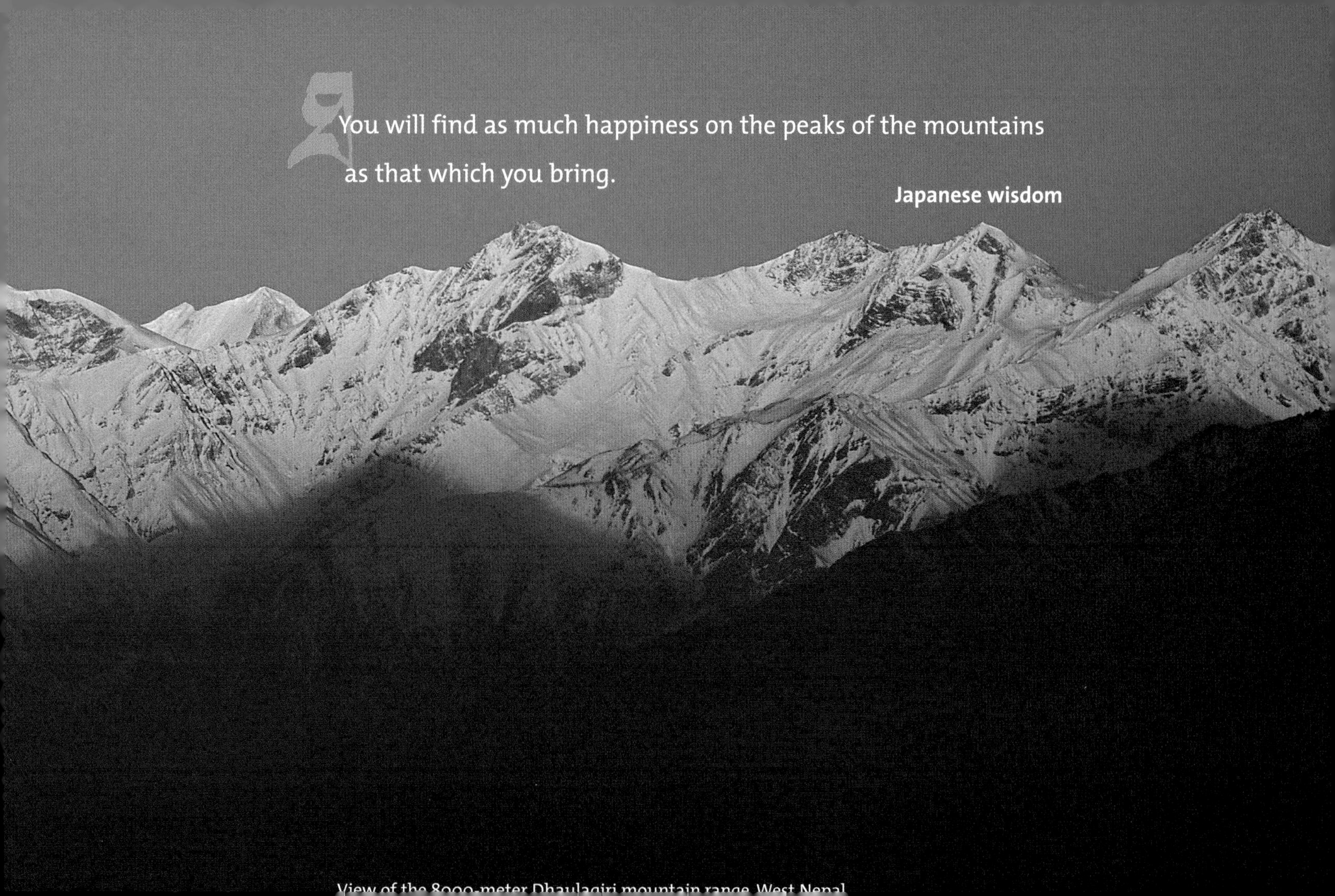

View of the 8000-meter Dhaulagiri mountain range, West Nepal

How I am is much more important than what I have.

Phil Bosmans

Ani Chemi Zong, a nun of the Bon religion from Narchu in North Tibet, on the 17th day of circumambulating Mt. Kailash by full-length prostration.

Today is the first day of the rest of my life; what shall I do with it?

Ayya Khema

Peasant woman Tashi overlooking her barley field, Lingshed, Ladakh.

Again and again: the main practice is to take your time!

Take your time to listen, to hold hands, to enjoy the scent of a rose,

to admire the twilight …

Matthias Stöbener

Peasant girl in the Terai, Nepal.

Before enlightenment:

Chop wood, carry water.

After enlightenment:

Chop wood, carry water.

Zen proverb

Peasant in his field near Kathmandu, Nepal.

You cannot explore the universe in the same way as you can explore yourself. Realize yourself; then you realize the universe.

Mahatma Gandhi

Three Sadhus in the morning time, Pashupatinath, Kathmandu, Nepal.

If in our everyday life we smile, remain peaceful and happy, this does not only help ourselves, but everybody else, too.

If we really know what it means to live, we can hardly begin the day in a better way than with a smile, can we?

Our smile encourages our awareness and our resolve to live in peace and joy. The source of a true smile is an awakened mind.

Thich Nhat Hanh

Nepali porters in Rolwaling valley, East Nepal.

As hard as yesterday may have been, it is important that you can make a new start today. Our body is a precious gift; we should take good care of it. For it is the place of our awakening and of our enlightenment. Hold your body upright, breathe deeply, and relax; then your life energy can flow.

From the Jatakas

Little Susma skillfully cutting up green squash, Ghasa, West Nepal.

I get to know people, not religions, colors of the skin, or races.

Konrad Thurano

Fully concentrated and with all their effort, the children and grown-ups of Bhaktapur are pulling the shrine carriage through the streets, Nepal.

Happiness is not a place but a direction!

Sogyal Rinpoche

Silhouette of Janakpur, South Nepal.

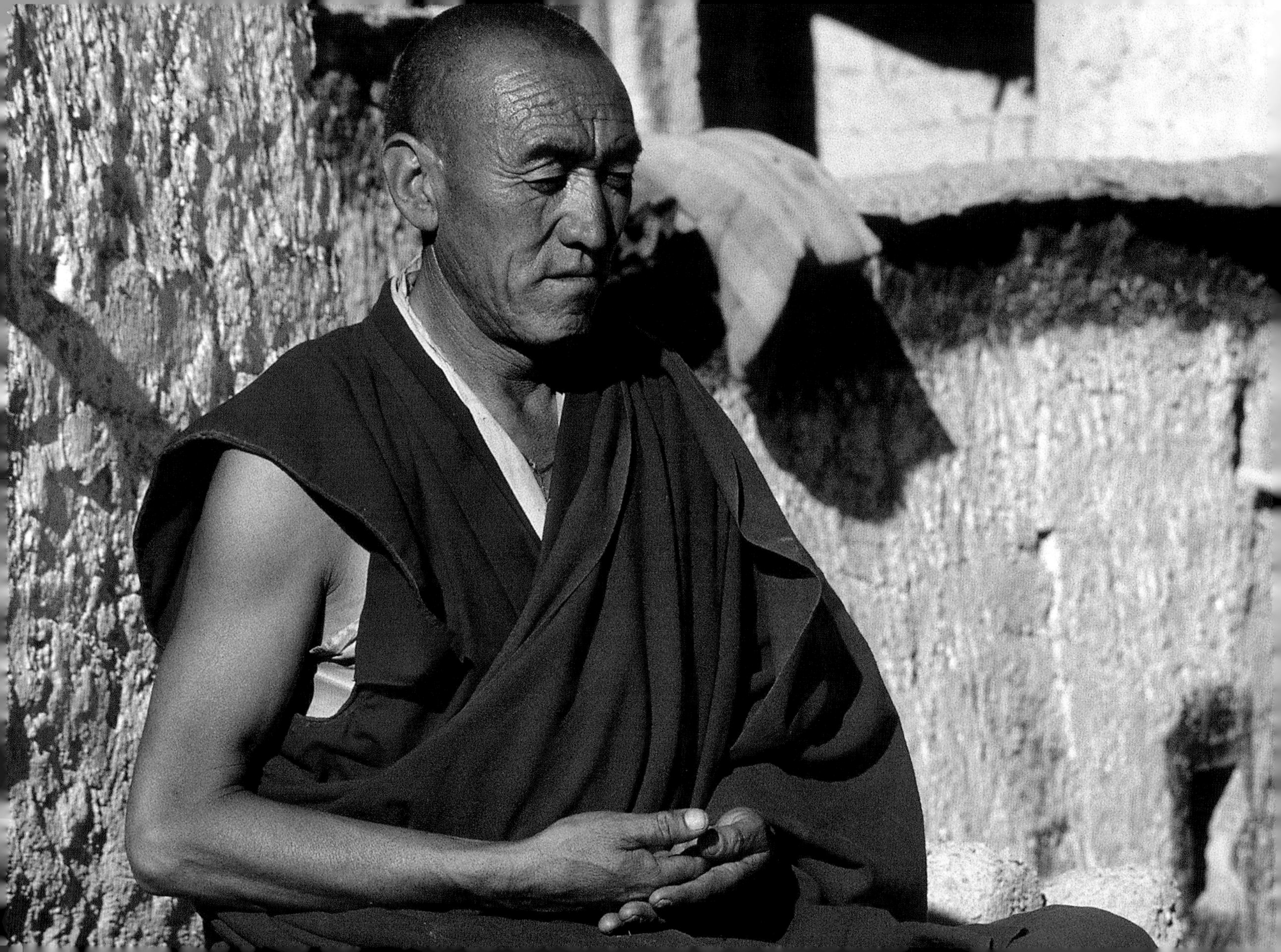

Meditation

The umbrella casts its protective shield on the one who carries it, protects him from disease, suffering, evil, and other obstacles, like the heat of passion. Whereas the stick supporting the umbrella's roof symbolizes the world's axis, the roof itself stands for wisdom, and the side hangings stand for compassion. Once a royal attribute reserved for few people of nobility and reputation, enhancing honor and respect, the umbrella of the doctrine gives protection from all evil to those who aim at liberation through the practice of meditation.

In meditation we meet the divine ground; we move a little bit closer to the center of life. We practice to let go and to relax; all our inner disease comes to an end. We experience where our roots are, where we could find shelter. This is the path to truth and enlightenment; we reach liberation from many restraints.

From the Dhammapada

Sunrise at the Potala Palace, Lhasa, Tibet.

I breathe in and I know that fury makes me ugly.

I breathe out and I wish not to be distorted by fury.

I breathe in and I know that I have to take care of myself.

I breathe out and I know that sympathetic compassion is the only answer.

Thich Nhat Hanh

Morning atmosphere at the steps leading up to Svayambunath Stupa, Kathmandu Valley, Nepal.

All suffering arises from man's inability to sit still and remain by himself.

Anthony de Mello

Tibetan nomad on his way to Mt. Kailash, West Tibet.

To meditate means to see the sun of the mind rise after a night of visitation, of tempest and thunderstorm for the soul. If you wish to have a fresh look at the world, learn to meditate.

Indian wisdom

Old peasant performing prostrations to Avalokiteshvara, the Buddha aspect of compassion, Braga Monastery, Annapurna region, West Nepal.

Meditation does not mean clinging to, identifying with or taking possession of something. All of this only leads to suffering. Meditation means looking, watching, becoming aware, understanding. It leads to scrutinizing love.

Anthony de Mello

Tibetan mother with her one-year-old son on kora around the Jokhang Temple in Lhasa, Tibet.

新世纪大厦

Mani stone and prayer flags at Mt. Kailash, West Tibet.

The trees, the flowers, the herbs: silently they grow.

The stars, the sun, the moon: silently they move.

Silence gives us a different view on things.

Mother Teresa

Mani stone on a wintry path in the land of the sherpa, Khumbu, Nepal.

Do not fear loneliness if it comes to you.

It is an opportunity to find yourself and to make you strong.

Drukpa Rinpoche

Prayer flags and chorten on the way to Tengpoche Monastery, Khumbu, Nepal.

To practice walking meditation really means to enjoy walking – no walking to arrive somewhere, but walking for the sake of walking. There is no other purpose than to be in the present moment, intentionally to feel the breath and the walking, and to enjoy every step.

Thich Nhat Hanh

Hindu pilgrim on his way back from Muktinath, Kali Gandaki canyon, West Nepal.

The word meditation does not just mean thinking, reflecting, examining, looking, and pondering; in Sanskrit it has another, much deeper meaning – measuring, in the sense of becoming.

Krishnamurti

Sadhu Rade Baba on a rock in Gosaikunde Lake, North Nepal.

Silence: this is returning to one's designation.

Returning to one's designation: this is eternity.

To realize eternity: this is wisdom.

They, who do not realize eternity, act blindly and inauspiciously.

Realization of eternity brings forbearance.

Laotse

Brahmin Shiva taking a rest at a moss-covered wall in Pashupatinath, Nepal.

The vast open dimension of the view, mind in its natural being is like space – no center, no edge, no reference point.

Shabkar

Scenery on the way to Lo Mantang in the Upper Mustang area, Nepal.

In western civilization we have well understood to act, but forgotten to be.
Therefore hardly anybody in the west can deal with silence and solitude.

Matthias Stöbener

View over the Kumbum chorten in Gyantse, Tibet.

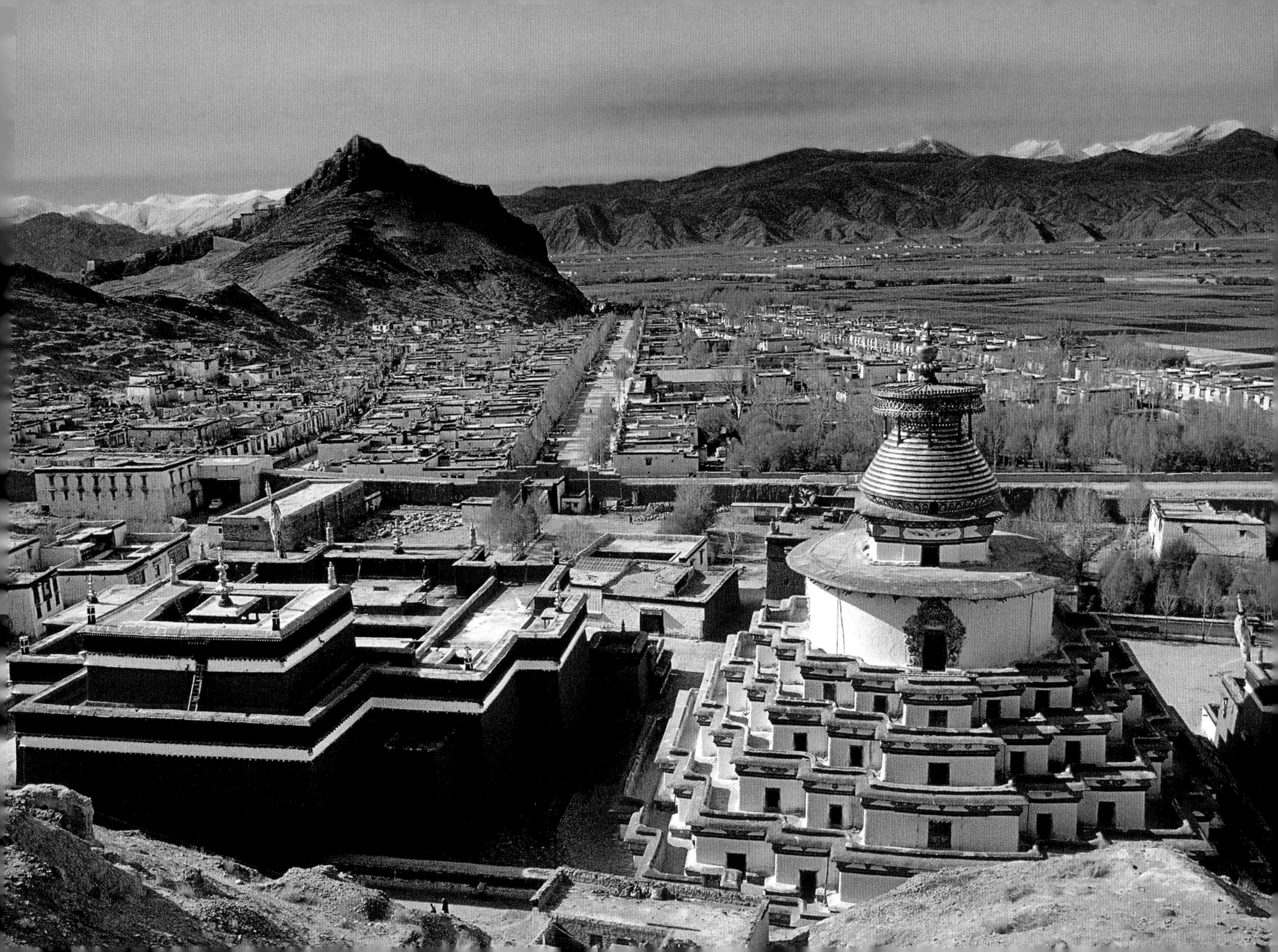

You can meditate traveling by bus, or having a walk in the forest full of light and shadow, or listening to the singing of the birds, or beholding your wife's or your child's face.

Krishnamurti

Peasant Tashi Wangdu and his wife Tashi separating the wheat from the chaff, Lingshed, North India.

When you are in this state of limitless openness,
relax into its open dimension; remain in this openness,
become one with this state; then, completely naturally,
you will let go more and more – wonderful!

Dilgo Khyentse Rinpoche

Peasant woman on a field near Ghasa, West Nepal.

If you let the muddy water settle,

it will get clear.

If you let your agitated mind settle,

your behavior likewise will become clear.

Buddha Shakyamuni

Old Sadhu Hanuman Baba drying his hair on a hot stone, West Nepal.

Stop accumulating things, if you want to lead a successful life.
The accumulation of material goods is just a caricature of happiness.
It splits up and encumbers the mind. Become light once more!

Drukpa Rinpoche

Fossils in a riverbed of the Himalayas, Nepal.

Striving after the worldly, and the path to nirvana –
these are two roads leading into different directions.

From the Dhammapada

Tibetan pilgrims prostrating at the old main entrance of the Jokhang temple in Lhasa, Tibet.

There is no thought other than emptiness. Recognizing their empty nature in the moment they arise, thoughts dissolve. Then desire and hatred cannot disturb the mind anymore. Disturbing emotions collapse by themselves. As no more negative action is accumulated, no more suffering will follow.

Dilgo Khyentse Rinpoche

Tibetan Dawa visiting Tashilunpo Monastery in Shigatse, Tibet.

When the five senses and the mind are calm and the thinking intellect remains in stillness, the highest path is entered.

From the Upanishads

Sadhu Muni Baba performing his morning Yoga exercises, Terrai, South Nepal.

The gift of learning to meditate is the greatest gift you can give yourself in this life. For it is only through meditation that you can undertake the journey to discover your true nature, and so find the stability and confidence you will need to live, and die, well; Meditation is the road to enlightenment.

Sogyal Rinpoche

Young monk in Rumtek Monastery, Sikkim.

May all beings experience happiness and the causes of happiness;
may they all be free from suffering and the causes of suffering;
may they never be separated from the supreme happiness, which is free from suffering;
may they all live in equanimity without too much attachment and too much aversion;
and may they live in the knowledge of the sameness of everything that lives.
Buddhist verses of dedication

Glossary

Amitabha
One of the five Mahayana meditation buddhas having derived from the Primordial Buddha. Amitabha is regarded as the source of light and life.

Bardo
State between death and rebirth. According to Tibetan thinking the mind remains in this state for 49 days.

Bodhisattva
A practitioner of Mahayana or Vajrayana on the path to enlightenment. Appearance of an enlightened being assisting others to cope with their lives.

Bon
Pre-Buddhist popular belief in Tibet. A natural religion characterized by animist and magical elements.

Chorten
Buddhist relic shrine.

Dhammapada
Ancient Buddhist text containing the essence of the Buddha's doctrine.

Dharma
The doctrine taught by the Buddha.

Jainism
Indian religion promulgated by Vardhamana Mahavira about 500 BC, according to which the world is not governed by a creator god, but by the laws of the cosmos and of morality.

Karma
Skt. "action"; causality of recompense; prerequisite for further existences.

Kora
Ritual circumambulation of sacred sites.

Lama
Spiritual teacher in the Tibetan tradition.

Mandala
Two or three-dimensional arrangement of symbols representing the power of consciousness.

Mantra
Ancient Buddhist meditation formula which is repeated many times and is considered to protect the mind from negative thinking.

Nirvana
Liberation from the cycle of life, death, and rebirth – the painful circle of existences.

Om mani padme hum
Literally roughly: "Precious jewel in the lotus flower." The mantra is considered to be the most commonly recited in the world. Its meaning is about the unity of wisdom and method.

Padmasambhava
Skt. "Lotus born." Through his ability to subdue spirits and demons, Padmasambhava prepared the ground for the Buddhist doctrine in the Himalaya region.

Rinpoche
"Precious one;" title of a reincarnated lama.

Sadhu
Skt. "good one." Term for ascetic Hindu saint or monk.

Samsara
Skt. "journey." Cyclic existence of all beings caused by karma, and perceived as suffering.

Samyutta Nikaya
"Compiled Collection," third part of the Suttapitaka ("Basket of Lectures") of Theravada Buddhism; talks, lectures, and discussions of the Buddha and of his various followers; compiled probably in the third century BC.

Sutta Nipata
Collection of early Buddhist doctrinal poetry.

Tantra
Term for the scriptures of Vajrayana and Tantrayana.

Tara
Most important female meditation deity and bodhisattva representing supreme compassion.

Upanishads
Final part of the Vedas composed between 800 and 400 BC; the Upanishads are counted among the oldest philosophical texts of India.

Vajrayana
Kind of Tantrism mainly practiced in the Tibetan cultural world.

Short biographies

Anthony de Mello
1931-1987
Born in Bombay; philosophical, theological, and psychological studies after having entered the Jesuit order; connects spirituality of the east with western wisdom traditions; wisdom teacher.

Ayya Khema
1923-1997
As a child of Jewish parents, she emigrated from Germany at the age of fifteen; ordained as a Buddhist nun in the Theravada tradition at the age of 56.

Buddha
Literally: "the awakened one;" enlightened being having overcome the cyclic existences of suffering. Siddhartha Gautama, born in Lumbini, Nepal, 560 BC, attained enlightenment under the bodhi tree in Bodghaya, India; Buddha Shakyamuni is considered the founder of the Buddhist religion; the Buddha, the Dharma (the doctrine of the Buddha), and the Sangha (the community of followers) are the three objects of refuge (three jewels) of practicing Buddhists.

Dalai Lama
"Ocean of Wisdom;" title of honor given to the secular and religious leader of Tibet by the Mongols in 1578; the transmission lineage of the Dalai Lamas has been uninterrupted until today.

Dilgo Khyentse Rinpoche
1910-1991
Buddhist master of the Nyingma tradition.

Drukpa Rinpoche
1989†
Tibetan master with close relations to the Dalai Lama; escaped from Tibet in 1959; then taught in Dharamsala, later in Nepal.

Jean-Francois Revel
Born 1924;
philosopher and agnostic; Matthieu Ricard's father.

Jiddu Krishnamurti
1895-1986
Indian Brahmin, philosopher, and scholar.

Kalu Rinpoche
1905-1989
Meditation master of the Tibetan Buddhist tradition; went to India escaping from the Chinese invasion of Tibet; taught in Asia, Europe, and North America.

Khalil Gibran
1883-1931
Poet, philosopher, and artist; born in the Lebanon; emigrated to the U.S. when he was young; his work is dedicated to the reconciliation of the Western and Arab worlds.

Mahatma Gandhi
1869-1948
Indian lawyer and human rights activist who worked for the independence of India.

Marc Aurel
(Marcus Aurelius Antonius)
121-180
Roman emperor from 161; philosopher (late eclectic Stoicism).

Matthieu Ricard
Born 1946 in France; biologist; has lived in the Himalaya region since 1972; student of Dilgo Khyentse Rinpoche; Buddhist monk, photographer, and translator of the 14th Dalai Lama.

Matthias Stöbener
Freelance writer resident in Augsburg, Germany; member of a catholic monastic order; working on the Buddhist tradition.

Milarepa
1040-1123
Tibetan yogi; disciple of the Tibetan lama Marpa (1012-1098) who established the Kagyu school in Tibet. Milarepa had to undergo great hardship imposed by Marpa before he was initiated to the doctrine.

Mother Teresa
1910-1997
Nobel Peace prize laureate in 1979; catholic nun of Albanian origin; Indian citizen from 1947; founded the Missionaries of Charity order in 1950.

Phil Bosmans
Priest in a catholic order; initiator of the "Movement without a Name" founded in Belgium in 1959, a movement for more humanity in the modern world.

Rabindranath Tagore
1861–1941
Writer, painter, musician; native of Bengal; took up studies in England at the age of 17; Tagore was friends with Mahatma Gandhi.

Shantideva
Bodhisattva and representative of the Middle Way philosophy in eighth century India.

Sogyal Rinpoche
Lama of the Nyingma school teaching in the west; renowned author.

Swami Prajnanpad
1891-1974
Follower of Gandhi; teacher of physics, English literature, and Indian philosophy in Benares; Swami Prajnanpad considered Freud's psychoanalysis to be the link between the Upanishads and everyday life.

Thich Nhat Hanh
Born 1926; Vietnamese meditation master living in exile in France; considered an important representative of Buddhism in the west.

Vincent de Paul
1581–1660
Catholic priest engaged in charity and nursing the sick; sainted in 1737 by Pope Clemens XII; founder of the "Congregation of the Merciful Sisters."

Wolfgang Wenger
Born 1962; Austrian writer; studies of German language and literature, as well as religious instruction.

23-year-old Bon pilgrim Longdo Chamzen from Amdo touching a holy mani stone on the way to Dirapuk Monastery, Mt. Kailash, West Tibet.

Further Reading

Harvey Arden (ed.), Noble Red Man: Lakota Wisdomkeeper, Atria Books/Beyond Words, 1994
Ayya Khema, Be An Island: The Buddhist Practice of Inner Peace, Wisdom Publications, 1999
Brandon Bays, The Journey: A Practical Guide to Healing Your Life and Setting Yourself Free, Atria 2002
Phil Bosmans, Whispering Hope, Hyperion Books; New Ed edition 1990
Dalai Lama, The Art of Happiness: A Handbook for Living, Riverhead Hardcover 1998
Dalai Lama, How to Practice : The Way to a Meaningful Life, Atria 2001
Dalai Lama, The Universe in a Single Atom: The Convergence of Science and Spirituality, Broadway 2006
Dalai Lama, Ethics for the New Millennium, Riverhead Trade, 2001
Drukpa Rinpoche et al., The Heart Treasure of the Enlightened Ones: The Practice of View, Meditation, and Action: A Discourse Virtuous in the Beginning, Middle, and End, Shambhala; 1st ed edition 1993
Albert Einstein, Out of My Later Years Through His Own Words, Castle Books; Revised edition 2005
D. and O. Föllmi, Wisdom: 365 Thoughts from Indian Masters (Offerings for Humanity), Harry N. Abrams 2004
Erich Fromm, The Art of Loving, Harper Perennial Modern Classics; 15 Anv edition 2006
Mahatma Gandhi/Richard Attenborough, The Words of Gandhi, Newmarket Press; 2 edition 2001
Khalil Gibran, Visions of the Prophet, Frog Books 1997
Andrew Harvey, Teachings of Rumi, Shambhala; 1st ed edition 1999
Susan Hayward, A Guide for the Advanced Soul: A Book of Insight (Guide for the Advanced Soul), Little Brown and Company; 1st American ed edition 1995
Hildegard of Bingen: Secrets of God: Writings of Hildegard of Bingen, Shambhala; 1 edition 1996
Devdutt Pattanaik, Shiva – An Introduction, Vakils Feffer & Simons Ltd; 2nd Rep edition 1997
Confucius, The Analects, translated and annotated by Arthur Waley, Macmillan 1938
Jack Kornfield, Buddha's Little Instruction Book, Bantam Books 1994
Norma Levine, A Yearbook of Buddhist Wisdom, Quest Books 1996
Sri Ramakrishna: Sayings of Sri Ramakrishna, Ramakrishna Math 2004
Jean-Francois Revel & Matthieu Ricard, The Monk and the Philosopher: A Father and Son Discuss the Meaning of Life, Schocken; Reprint edition 2000
Matthieu Ricard: Journey to Enlightenment, Aperture 1996
Rainer Maria Rilke, Selected poems of Rainer Maria Rilke, Harper & Row; 1st ed edition 1981
Peter Gay and Walter Kaufmann, Basic Writings of Nietzsche (Modern Library Classics), Modern Library; Modern Library edition 2000
Walpola Rahula, What the Buddha Taught: Revised and Expanded Edition with Texts from Suttas and Dhammapada, Grove Press; First Evergreen Edition edition 1974
Sogyal Rinpoche, The Tibetan Book of Living and Dying, Random House 1992
Sogyal Rinpoche, Glimpse After Glimpse, San Francisco 1995
Mutter Teresa, In My Own Words, Gramercy 1997
Mutter Teresa, Come Be My Light, Doubleday, 2007

The renowned Yogi Milarepa of the Kagyu school has meditated for years at Mt. Kailash.

Dieter Glogowski having arrived at Lingshed Monastery.

Acknowledgements

I am very grateful to the 14th Dalai Lama for his support and his trust in my work. Furthermore I would like to express my thanks to Franz Binder, writer and Himalaya expert, for his advice and for the introduction to this book; to my wife Annette Jungmichel for helping to compile the quotations; to Yeshe Osel for the Tibetan calligraphy; to Sabrina Schäfer for her camera assistance. Many thanks to all the people in the Himalaya region who have been accompanying my work so caringly for 25 years, namely Geshe Lama Ngawang Changchup, Karma Namgyal, Shiva Shrestha, Tashi and Dolma Lama, Tenzing Thinley, Rade Baba, and Shiva Brahman. Thank you very much to the sponsors who have actively supported my projects for many years: Manfred Hell, Miriam Arndt, Markus Pieker (Jack Wolfskin); Christine Alig (Austrian Airlines); Michael Schott, Manfred Häupl (Hauser Exkursionen); Steffen Keil (Leica); Maike Reinhardt (Kodak); Christoph Schleidt (Ortlieb). This book is dedicated to my mother Gisela, who has given my mind a lot of space and has guided me with her loving care.

Publication Note

Photography and compilation of quotations: Dieter Glogowski
Introduction: Franz Binder, Munich, Germany
Design: Werner Poll, Munich,
revised by Agnes Meyer-Wilmes, Munich, Germany,
Calligraphy: Yeshe Osel
Translation: Hannelore Wenderoth, Bad Camberg, Germany
Proof reading: Brian Leonard, Bad Goisern, Austria
Product management for the English edition: Dr. Birgit Kneip
Production: Bettina Schippel
Repro: Repro Ludwig, Zell am See, Austria
Printed in Slowenia by MKT, Ljubljana

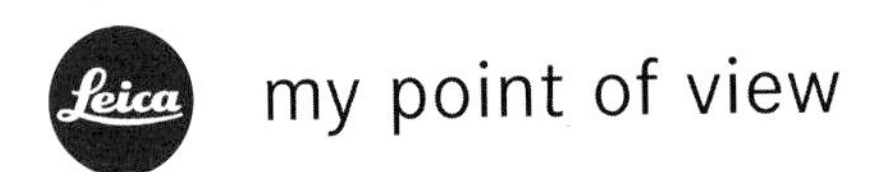

ISBN 978-3-7658-1733-5